MW00463125

KINDEZI :
The Kôngo Art
of
Babysitting

KINDEZI :
The Kôngo Art
of
Babysitting

K. Kia Bunseki Fu-Kiau

And

A. M. Lukondo-Wamba

INPRINT EDITIONS
Baltimore

KINDEZI

Copyright © 1988 by K. Kia Bunseki Fu-Kiau
Introduction Copyright © 2000 by Marimba Ani
Published 2000 by INPRINT EDITIONS, Baltimore
All Rights Reserved.
Cover Design by Carles Juzang
ISBN-13 978-1-58073-025-9
ISBN-10 1-58073-025-6

ABOUT INPRINT EDITIONS

Our mission is to keep good books in print. We give life to books that might never be published or republished by making them available On Demand. Manuscripts and books are scanned, stored, and then printed as single or multiple copies from our digital library. When reprinting out-of-print books, we always use the best copy available.

INPRINT EDITIONS are especially useful to scholars, students, and general readers who have an interest in enjoying all that books have to offer. Our books are also a valuable resource for libraries in search of replacement copies.

Order INPRINT EDITIONS from:
Black Classic Press
P.O. Box 13414
Baltimore, MD 21203

Printed by BCP Digital Printing

Kindezi: The Kôngo Art of Babysitting
An Introduction
by Marimba Ani

In his ground-breaking work *Self-Healing Power and Therapy*, Dr. Fu-Kiau tells us that muntu (the human being), the "living sun," is perceived as a "power," "a phenomenon of perpetual veneration from conception to death" and beyond. Kindezi is about the process of how this "living sun" is nurtured once he/she has been brought into the physical world. The task of caring for this sacred muntu is the most important responsibility in Afrikan civilization.

Dr. Fu-Kiau intentionally translates Kindezi as the art of "babysitting" to shock us. My immediate impression upon reading the subtitle of his book was to question him, respectfully pointing out what seemed to be a mistaken translation—a poor choice of an English term. Dr. Fu-Kiau's response was given in his characteristically soft, patient, and considerate manner, which forces one to hang on his every word, convinced that wisdom is about to be bestowed. He explained that in European culture "babysitting" is thought to be an insignificant activity—a job for the least important people in our society. We know that "teenagers," who supposedly have nothing important to do, are given this task, and Afrikan women are imported from the Caribbean to care of European-American children as a testament to our alleged racial inferiority. Yet, according to the authors of this book, Kindezi is the greatest honor that can be bestowed upon a person in Afrikan society.

Fu-Kiau is bringing home the point, in a sharply critical manner, that while childhood is devalued in European society, Afrikan civilization is child-centered. This becomes clear as we understand human life in the context of spiritual community: a never-ending process of growth, development, transformation and accountability. The well-being of the community depends on the health and wholeness, the successful maturation of the persons who constitute its membership.

Kindezi, then, is an art that is focused not only on the nurturing of the young within the society, but on the growth of the ndezi (the caretaker, one who practices the art of Kindezi). In other words, as one develops the skills of Kindezi, one develops oneself as well. The ndezi must help the muntu, the "living sun," to "shine" (6); and, in the process, he/she learns how to "shine" with the power of a living sun. Because this process is continuous, the highest Kindezi (experience of service to the community) rests with the elders. Elders in Afrikan society are those who have become physically more frail, but who are spiritually stronger because they have grown further in personal development and have moved closer to the Ancestors, to the spiritual world and to the "Source of Life" itself (Kalunga). An "elder" is not just an "old person," but is someone still "mentally and spiritually strong and wise enough not only to maintain the community united but, above all, to build the moral foundation of the community youth and of generations to come" (9-10).

The Afrikan art and practice of Kindezi places great importance on the presence of "elders" in the community and their responsibility for the health and wholeness of the group. By linking the elders to the youth of the society, the concept stresses intergenerational continuity, meaningful communication, consistency of value formation and transmission, and mutual responsibility and accountability. This brings us to the contemporary relevance of this book.

The greatest challenge that faces people of Afrikan descent displaced from our grounding in the Motherland is social fragmentation, disconnectedness and axiological or value confusion. The spiritual strength of our enslaved Ancestors brought us through the brutal and inhumane disruption of the Maafa. They did this by finding ways to raise their children and teach them values. Indeed the only source of resistance available to us was the strength of our spirit—our

"Soul-Force" (Leonard Barrett)—which we used to continually recreate community. This sense of community was always a strong and powerful force on which Afrikan descendants have depended during the major historical periods of our saga in this forced Diaspora. Since the 1960's, however, which appeared on the surface to bring what many thought were political and economic gains, our cultural consciousness has deteriorated. The importance of family has diminished in our minds, and the increased exposure to the destructive forces of American society has successfully eaten away at the fabric of our social institutions.

Our youth, on whom we depend for the future development, vindication, and strength of our community, are stolen from us by an arsenal of intellectual and cultural poisons. They are spiritually attacked from before birth with the weapons of an anti-Afrikan environment. We lack true "elders" because they themselves have not been taken through a process of cultural development. Those "elders" that we do have are discarded and relegated to the garbage heaps of a capitalist society, which values only that which brings material gain. Since babies are regarded as burdens that do not add anything materially to the group, they also become peripheral to significant endeavors. "Babysitting," therefore, is one of the least valued tasks in our cluttered lives, and elders become "useless" embarrassments. We have imitated Euro-American decadence until we no longer recognize basic Afrikan values. Kindezi provides an answer for a people in crisis, an antidote to chronic "cultural misorientation" (Kambon).

Dr. Fu-Kiau and his co-author Psychologist Lukondo-Wamba bring us ancient wisdom from our Ancestral home in the form of Kindezi. The necessity of a focus on the nurturing of young children and the value of our Elder-Teachers is a simple, but not simplistic, truth. It is the process (dingo-dingo) through which "social patterns" are transferred to "the community's youngest members" (1). Kindezi is a critical ingredient of the anti-viral serum needed to combat our condition of "cultural AIDS." It is the basic process of Afrikan socialization. We are talking about the reconstruction of the family in its most fundamental and dynamic sense.

Kindezi is about using the spiritual, mental, and cultural strength of our elders to contribute to the process of developing generations of culturally healthy youth, who grow to become powerful elders, who then in turn, produce culturally healthy youth, and so on for millennia to come.

While the system of Kindezi is an ancient one, it took on greater importance during the period in which the Bakongo people were fighting against the impending onslaught of European colonial domination. Women had to be freed to fight alongside of their men, often leading the community in battle themselves. The art of Kindezi allowed them to do so without sacrificing the care and socialization of their children. Fu-Kiau and Lukondo-Wamba go on to explain that Afrikan women have always been "farmers" spending long hours away from their children. According to the authors, it was Kindezi that allowed Afrikan women to be "liberated" so that they could meaningfully contribute to the economic welfare of the family. This, they claim, is where European women got their concept of "women's lib" because such models were lacking in the patriarchy of their own cultural history.

In the brief statement contained in these pages, Fu-Kiau and Lukondo-Wamba team up to present a surprisingly thorough description of the Afrikan socialization process. The book focuses on the importance of elders in Afrikan society in relationship to the importance of Afrikan Youth. Socially, elders teach and they give counsel, so they give children a sense of their history and explain to them the meaning of "the path of life" and their importance in the life of the community (11). Economically, elders help to contribute to the well-being and vibrance of the community by performing the vital function of Kindezi. In this way, they remain useful and reciprocally are taken care of with special attention to their physical and emotional well-being. The authors draw attention to the profound depth of the Afrikan understanding of the human spirit, explaining that because elders in traditional Afrikan society feel useful they are (or were before Afrikans began abandoning Afrikan ways) less likely to suffer from "psychosomatic" illness and unnecessary biophysical deterioration (11). Meanwhile, more and more Afrikan elders in the Diaspora are suffering from Alzheimer's and other forms of dementia, which totally debilitate them and cause them unwillingly to become a burdensome responsibility for the adult members of the family. Our authentic culture is spiritually based; thus its disintegration causes spiritual and therefore physical destruction. However, the authors have presented us with a model for contemporary cultural healing.

The practical value of this book is immense. Fu-Kiau and Lukondo-Wamba explain Kindezi in terms of its social, economic, and political significance. In this regard, this small book has great value in the development of an Afrikan-centered pedagogy. The approach of teaching through song is discussed at some length, a method that has traditionally spoken to the spirit of Afrikan children, but is only now being acknowledged in European pedagogical theory. The authors explain how language—the powerful energizing force of Afrika—becomes the effective and affective tool of pedagogy through the art of Kindezi.

The answer to Afrikan cultural reconstruction lies in Sankofa, the reclamation of those processes which become the threads of our mended cultural quilt. Kindezi is a most valuable primer for Afrikan-centered (re)socialization, the healing of the Afrikan family, and Afrikan cultural reconstruction. You have picked up the right book. It tells you how to teach your children (and yourself) **TO BE AFRIKAN!**

CONTENTS

I. THE CONCEPT OF KINDEZI

One may wonder what is "Kindezi"? Is it a concept? A field of interest? What is it for the people of Africa and the Kôngo, in particular?

Kindezi, the art of babysitting, is an old art among Africans, in general, and the Bântu, in particular. It is basically the art of touching, caring for, and protecting the child's life and the environment, *kinzungidila*, in which the child's multidimensional development takes place. The word "Kindezi," a Kikôngo language term, stems itself from the root verb *lela*,[1] which means to enjoy taking and giving special care.

To babysit—*lela*, i.e., to give special care—is, first of all, a way of transferring social patterns to the community's youngest members. And, secondly, it is the child's orientation for life which comprises very well-determined directions according to community norms and values. As such, the Kindezi/Kindesi may vary from one society to another with respect to individual systems and their values.

Kindezi, the art of babysitting, also provides one with the opportunity to witness a personal living experience throughout the process of development of the most delicate stage of life: that of the child.

Because of these philosophical views about Kindezi among African people and the Kôngo in particular, babysitting is considered to be a therapeutic method highly recommended in helping old people (while using them as babysitters) deal with their diverse social, psychological, and/or gerontologically-related problems. For young babysitters the Kindezi is seen as a social preadaption/preparation toward fatherhood/motherhood responsibilities. It is also programmed for this last group as a learning experience for life and a way of acquiring the forbearance that makes for good mothers and good fathers. Very often young couples without children are required, in the Kôngo society, to babysit for community members (extended family) as a preparation for the coming of their own children.

Babysitting is an experience required of all community members in the African world, no matter what their physical state may be. Understanding the *dingo-dingo* (process) of child development is one of the basic and most important principles in the understanding of the value and respect of life. *Walèmbwa lela kalèndi bakula ntoko za môyo ngâtu za buta mu zola ko*— "Whoever never babysat," says a Kôngo proverb, "will never understand the beauty of life nor that of parenting with love."

Historically speaking, Kindezi has existed in Africa since time immemorial, but its real development began during the precolonial period when mothers, without any exception, were obliged to take arms like their fellow men, not only to fight against the invasion of their territories, but also to lead the wars.[2] The development of Kindezi for these purposes continued on and became common during colonization with the introduction of new crops in Africa that required enormous effort and time for cultivation. This was a time during which both father and mother were "transformed" to beasts of burden by the world-exploiting powers under the cover of the "civilized mission." Both men and women worked for the "corvée" (forced and free labor) in the creation of roads, conveyance, production of products of exportation, and so on. Mothers and fathers were unable to take care of their children as they had been accustomed to. The burden, consequently, fell upon old people's shoulders and/or upon the youngest ones who were below the recruiting age for the corvée.

It is the creation of this hardest but most beautiful art,

2

Kindezi, or the art of caring for the child's life and the social environment into which this care and this development stem under such difficult, indeed, cruel circumstances, that we devote this study. The philosophical concepts of Kindezi described here are based upon Kôngo culture. This study is a product of a joint effort presented not only to our fellow Bakôngo people, but to all men and women in the field of Kindezi in communities throughout the entire world.

NOTES

1. Its variant is *leza*.
2. The African woman always has been involved in almost all activities of life: social, economic, as well as military. During the precolonial era she had been as her fellow man, a good general in the army. This is the case of Nzîng'a Matâmba and Vita-Kimpa in the ancient Kingdom of the Kôngo, who, as army generals, led the anticolonial war.

II. KINDS OF NDEZI

Though things are rapidly changing today in Africa, the Kindezi, in its substructure, still remains as a skill and an art to be learned by all young community members, girls as well as boys, through an initiatic and practical process for, as a Kôngo proverb would say, *Kindezi m'fuma mu kânda* (The art of babysitting is a *baobab* to the community), i.e., a strong supporter of community economic activities (Fig. 1). Babysitting, *sâla kindezi*, is not instinctively acquired as some would assume or pretend. *Dingo-dingo diena* it is a process by which one discovers the mystery of human growth and reaches the total understanding of the psychology of the child.

By babysitting, one learns the wonderful skill of being responsible for another life and how to become a new "living pattern." A "living pattern" is a model through which cultural values are transmitted from generation to generation. Through Kindezi, Africans acquire this skill, a skill that has made the African not only one of the most religious human beings on earth but, also, one of the most humanistic.

African parents, mothers in particular, have a great concern about their children's childhood because they are aware that *Kimbuta kia mûntu, bônso kimûntu, ĝa mataba*—"One's leadership, like one's personality, finds its roots in the childhood." Earlier events in the childhood life play an important role in adulthood. As such, great attention is paid to whoever has a role to play in the life of a child—the human being with the quickest copying mind. This basic understanding that child-

4

Fig. 1: *Kindezi, m'fuma mu kânda*—"the art of babysitting is a *baobab* to the community."

hood is the foundation which determines the quality of a society is the main reason that prompted African communities to make Kindezi an art, or *kinkete*, to be learned by all their members. Thus, Kindezi is required in societies that want to prepare their members to become not only good fathers and mothers, but, above all, people who care about life and who understand, both humanely and spiritually, the highly unshakable value of the human being that we all are. From this premise the Kindezi became a popular art and a personal living experience in earlier and later life; one leaves the world in the same state of physical weakness as one comes into it.

5

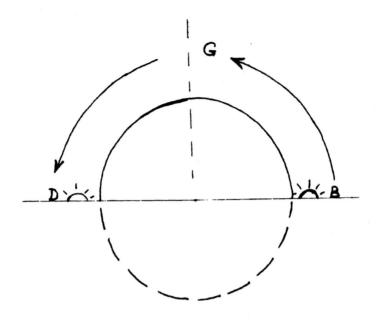

Fig. 2: The birth of a child is the raising of a "living sun":
B—the sunrise is its rising point (birth)
G—the sun trajectory is its direction of growth and changes
D—the sunset is its point of the highest change (death)

For the Bântu, in general, and the Kôngo, in particular, the coming of a child in the community is the rising of a new and unique "living sun" into it.[1] It is the responsibility of the community as a whole and of *ndezi*, in particular, to help this "living sun" to shine and grow in its earliest stage (Fig. 2).

Ndezi, the one who practices the art of Kindezi, the babysitter, is not to be confused with *n'sânsi*, the nurse girl. The former, ndezi, deals directly not with infants (babies), but with children and the care to be given to them. The latter, n'sânsi (nurse girl), whose art is Kinsânsi, deals not with children but with infants/babies and/or with nursing mothers and the care to be

6

given to them. An n'sânsi is a young lady or a girl appointed by the community or by the extended family members to go and live, for a few months, with a nursing mother to assist her in her delicate duty. Her job is basically linked to maternity. All n'sânsi (nurse girls) can babysit, but all ndezi (babysitters) cannot become nurse persons. A male is never, ethically, appointed to be a nurse person to a nursing mother. It is a moral taboo.

Kindezi, the art of babysitting, is one of the most important responsibilities shared by females and males alike in an African community. The following proverb, *Kindezi wasâdulwa; kindezi una sâdila* (Someone babysat for you; you will babysit for somebody else.), became the motto and cornerstone of this art.

A boy/girl has to babysit for his/her youngest brothers and sisters while a grandparent babysits for her/his grandchildren. Anyone in the community—brother, sister, cousin, grandmother, aunt, uncle, friend or a neighbor—can babysit for a community child for, so says this Kôngo proverb, *Mwâna mu ntûnda, zitu kia mûntu mosi; ku mbazi, wa babônsono*, meaning, "The child in the mother's womb is a burden of one person; outside (born), it belongs to everybody (in the community).[2]

Accordingly, as one ascends or descends the plateau of social manpower (C), one can distinguish three main categories from which most ndezi (babysitters) are found. The first category is made up of young ndezi and the second of old ndezi (Fig. 3). Besides these two main groups there is a third group, the group of occasional ndezi. From zero to five years of age the child lives a life of helplessness. S/he needs some help for her/his full development. This help comes either from the n'sânsi (nurse girl) who lives with the nursing mother (for children less than two years old), or from the group B, C, or D through Kindezi, before falling again into the group E of "old children" of over eighty years old. As the reader will see hereafter, each of the above-mentioned babysitting groups is different from one another.

7

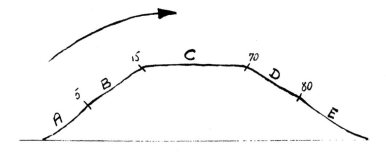

Fig. 3: Through growth, the "living sun" changes social roles and
statuses:
      A—stage of childhood with need of ndezi/babysitter
      B—stage of the child becoming a community ndezi
      C—stage of the "living sun" becomes a community pro-
         ductive force
      D—stage of the highest Kindezi (the experience to the
         service of the community)
      E—stage of the old-age childhood (the transition of the
         "living sun")

A. YOUNG NDEZI

A young ndezi is a person who is too young to be embodied
into social manpower. As such, s/he is not yet recognized as a
productive force within the community. Young babysitters
range between five and ten.

These young ndezi, being the group of growing people, constitute the most dynamic and energetic group of ndezi. They,
themselves, are in the stage of exploration of their own environment and, by babysitting for their younger brothers and sisters,
they help these latter to follow the path of the "dingo-dingo"
of life. The ndezi takes charge of the child all day long until
the night falls when the mother comes back home from her
tasks of the day. Children grow up greatly attached to their
ndezi, walking and playing nowhere but in the surroundings
of the village. The ndezi leave the village only to go to the river

to bathe themselves or the children for whom they are caring. On rare occasions, ndezi may have to take a persistently weeping child to its mother's workplace. They sometimes enjoy preparing meals, so that mothers will not have to cook after a long, hot day on the farm.[3]

Babysitting duties are numerous. S/he bounces the baby up and down on her/his back while crooning little cradle songs to soothe the infant. These songs have a great educative as well as psychological impact or influence on the child. We will see some of these songs in the next chapter.

The ndezi must also learn various techniques related to this art of babysitting: how to quiet or stop a weeping child; how to feed a child and what to do when the child goes astray while eating or drinking; how to hold the child while giving it a bath; how to tie the child on one's back; how to pull up (*sela*) or slide down (*tûlula/zelumuna*) a child tied on one's back, et cetera. Techniques related to the process of tying up (*kânga*) and untying (*kutula/vûla*) the child on one's back are only perfectly achieved by females. Young male ndezi prefer to run with their children seated on their necks, while young female ndezi will always have theirs tied up on their backs.

B. OLD NDEZI

Old babysitters are people who are excluded from the community force of production because of their age. They are too old to be embodied into social manpower. People with any physical disability are also included in this group.

Elder in Bântu societies in general, and the Kôngo in particular, constitute a powerful social force in the ancient art of Kindezi, the art without trace in the academic world. If old people are physically weak and can no longer participate economically as a productive force in the community, they are still mentally and spiritually strong and wise enough not only to maintain the community united but, above all, to build the moral foundation of the community youth and of generations

9

to come. An old person, like a young person, is considered in Africa to be a full part of the community, no matter how physically weak this person becomes. This person is never isolated from the society. Let us mention here, in passing, that among the Kôngo, as in many other Bântu societies, handicapped people, even those born severely retarded, are among the most accepted and almost deified mysteries in the community. No one, neither the king nor the *ngânga* (healer, scientist), has the right to end their right to be alive. Physical as well as mental "grayness," for Bântu people, is something to be proud of and younger generations aspire to it. A Kôngo proverb says: *Bitèta ku n'tu, milongi/mîna kalûnda* (Aging [to get gray hair] is not totally a negative thing.) "Grayness" is also a symbol of one who keeps community teaching/law, i.e., living and conforming with the law of dingo-dingo of life and change.

Nursing home, the one-way road travelled by those who never come back home, do not exist in traditional Bântu systems. If such nursing homes existed, they would be seen in African eyes and in the Kôngo in particular, as very negative institutions where their loved ones would not receive care, but would only sit or lie down, looking at the horizon of their approaching death. Further, such institutions would be seen as a monumental negative symbol of a careless society.

For the Kôngo, a proverb tells us: *Nuna i soba mbebe mu kânda* (To age is to change one's role/responsibility in the community). Aging is not a reason to isolate or kick someone out from the natural common path of *kala ye zima* (*being* while following the path of *extinguishing* slowly), and *dingo-dingo dia môyo ye nsobolo* (the process of life and change).

Because of this fundamental Bântu philosophy among the Kôngo towards their elders, old people with their lifelong experience as community members constitute the most important group of ndezi. These old people, thus, reenter the field of Kindezi, the art of babysitting, for social, economic, or humanitarian reasons.

10

Social Reasons

Elders are considered, among the Bântu people, as a special class with a special role within the community because of their special lifelong experience. As such, they are used in Kindezi not only as excellent ndezi—babysitters—themselves, but also as teachers and counselors to young ndezi. In these positions and roles as teachers, counselors, and ndezi, they have two main social duties to achieve: (1) to transfer into children's own language the history of the community to all children through songs, stories, legends, and games; and (2) to explain to these children the path of life, its meaning from *kala* (being, coming to be, to exist in this world) to *zima* (extinguishing, the death of the body for change), and the role of the community upon them.

Economic Reasons

Old people in Africa are used as babysitters—ndezi—to help the community with its children and other light duties while it is the responsibility of the community to take care of their needs by feeding, housing, clothing, and comforting them. We will come back to this point in the fourth chapter.

In addition to the reasons already mentioned, African old people are used as babysitters (ndezi) in their communities to deter psychosomatic ailments. With the effect of *luvèmba*, "the negative element that accumulates in our body through age (and which is the principal cause of a physical death[4])," old people weaken physically and return to the category of children—"old children." These old children may have had children of their own in the past. The absence of their own children may become a big problem, both physically and psychologically, at this particular moment of life. In this situation, African people do not want their elders to live in loneliness for, says Kôngo wisdom, *Bukaka n'sôngo; bulènda vônda*—"Loneliness is an illness, it can kill." As a therapeutic way of reducing psycholog-

11

ical and gerontologically related breakdowns, the Kôngo surround their elders, as community babysitters, with children to keep them busy. With this therapeutic technique, elders in the traditional Kôngo society happily end their last days of life. They literally die in the hands of their loved ones with respect and dignity after they have said to them, rather than to a nurse, their last word. This "last word" is the greatest thing any African person would expect from a dying loved one rather than prompting him/her to change or reword the will. It is believed that this "last word" far surpasses any material goods listed on a piece of paper called a testament or last will.

A Kôngo child learns a lot from an old ndezi of his/her community about plants, their names and uses, and where one can find them; about animals and moral stories related to them; what these animals eat and how they reproduce themselves; about people of afar, their customs, languages, and ways of life; and, above all, they learn what children like most: songs, stories, games, and tricks.

An old ndezi, for the children, is a star of life. They play, sing, jump, and dance with her/him. Her/his lap is the best bed to be in and rest. An old ndezi is sometimes seen as being better than one's own parents—mainly if this ndezi is a grandparent. S/he knows not only how to lull, but better, how to reproach a child. S/he is a parent par excellence for s/he knows what it is to be a parent, a ndezi/babysitter, and a child. And, above all, s/he is a person of experience who knows how to read people's minds.

C. OCCASIONAL NDEZI

Contrary to what is said about young and old ndezi, occasional ndezi (*ndezi yantôta*) are people on the plateau of social productive forces (Fig. 3). In other words, they are core producers of the community who for some reason have decided, for the day, to stay in the village to do certain tasks, such as: bake bread (*nika/yoka kwânga*), repair a house, extract palm oil (*kama mafuta*), wait for a visitor, et cetera. Under these conditions a parent (mother) may ask such an individual to babysit for her child while doing these other tasks. Such a babysitter is known as *ndezi yantôta* or *ndezi a bwèso*, meaning respectively and literally "windfall babysitter" and "babysitter by chance." This person serves as an ndezi while performing her/his other tasks on an ordinary schedule. Because of their divided attention between the child to watch over and the work to be done, problems, conflicts, and even accident can occur with the Kindezi practiced by this group. Consequently, a child, for example, might accidently crawl past the unattentive ndezi and fall into a fire or dumping hole. Many such accidents in Kindezi have occurred with the ndezi in this group. Many do not like to babysit for a child while occupied with another activity. It can be dangerous—even catastrophic—for the babysitter, as well as for the entire community, and may mean the loss of life for the child.

Occasional babysitting of this type is enjoyed and turns good only if there is more than one child around. These other children should be of different levels and ages so that they can keep an eye on one another for their own safety and protection.

Every African has, in one way or another, participated in one of the three different groups of ndezi for the simple reason that the social as well as cultural environment requires it. Everyone works for the community, and the community works for everyone. And with the practice of the Kindezi system, the youngest and the oldest members of the community are not excluded from the dingo-dingo (process) of collective economy. This explains why Kindezi, the art of babysitting, is not only the art of touching and caring for the child, but of shaping humankind and the future of its world environment.

NOTES

1. For more details on this subject read Fu-Kiau's *Cosmogonie-Kongo* (ONRD, Kinshasa, 1969), *The African Book Without Title*, and other of his works.

2. In Kôngo society parents never fight or kill each other because of their children. Children of together or divorced couples always belong to both parents and their respective communities. As such, a Mukôngo will never kidnap or kill his/her own child on the grounds of parental conflict.

3. Most farming women are busy on their farms from six o'clock in the morning to six o'clock in the evening.

4. See Fu-Kiau, *The African Book Without Title*, 1980.

III. CHILDREN IN THE HANDS OF THE NDEZI

A. WHO ARE THEY?

The children in the hands of the ndezi are all children of the community and from the community. They are the youngest members of the community, and represent the future of the community itself. Very often these children are familially related to one another.

Kôngo society pays great attention to its youth, for *Môyo a kânda, bilesi* (community life is in its youth) says a proverb. A community without youth has no future. But in order to insure a positive future, the community and all its members must take on the full responsibility for "initiating" (educating) its youth—*Bula mèso mâu*—as to their social, cultural, economic, and political responsibilities, be they communal, national, or international. To succeed in this task the *Mbôngi*, "community parliament,"[1] must create a good political atmosphere favorable to the cultural, social, economic, political, and intellectual growth of the youth. One way this is accomplished in Kôngo society is through the development of a very strong system of *ntungasani*, which can best be translated as "building wise individuals and strong community bonds through free and open critical debates." The Mbôngi is thus seen as the most popular school in the Kôngo system of education. Here all questions and matters related to community life are openly and commonly discussed. And, here in the Mbôngi, decisions are

15

made together in the community, by the community, for the community.

The ntungasani process in the Kôngo Mbôngi is even more democratic than the process of democracy in the West, for the simple reason that in this ntungasani process everyone in the community, absolutely everyone, participates in the process of making or changing an order or law.[2] Room for dictatorship simply does not exist. Thus, what children learn from their old ndezi stems from the Mbôngi, the community source of "official" information that gathers and builds up the communal society and its system.

B. WHAT DO THEY LEARN?

The *sâdulu*, (babysitting practical site/spot) does not contain a board to write on, nor a book to read. However, children in the sâdula "read" and receive a lot from the minds of their ndezi and so learn to "write" and assimilate much information about life in the community of the past, present, and of the future as well. The teaching is oral and practical. Children and their babysitters sometimes leave their sâdula site and move from one spot to another, visiting local blacksmiths, weavers, and potters. And very often they go collecting flowers, herbs, insects, roots, *bimènga* (pieces of pottery), eggs, mushrooms, rocks, bark, et cetera in and around the village. Learning the names and use of "things" in the child's environment is one of the most exciting stages in the sâdulu learning process. They learn how to carefully dissect small animals and insects. Through these experiences the child acquires a solid practical knowledge in matters related to anatomy, fauna, and flora. Additionally, these practical learning activities afford the children the opportunity to improve their native language development and increase their vocabularies.

Unfortunately, this solid knowledge of the mother tongue is disregarded in all modern African school systems, where there is no room for "nonscientific" African languages. This

16

belief that African languages are not equipped for modern scientific study is, in our point of view, foolish and a cancer on the body of African intellectual and economic growth.

The ndezi in the sâdulu holds to a rigid moral teaching with regard to community life matters. Here the experience of the old ndezi is expertly "poured" into the child, who then sings it, tastes it, feels it, and grasps it as her/his own.

It is in the sâdulu, the babysitting site, that the child learns the value of living, playing, singing, dancing, and laughing together with others no matter who they are and how rich or poor they might be. For the Bântu, and the Kôngo in particular, togetherness is something spiritual to be shared proudly with others. Togetherness is a power and energy that binds people and warms them up. Under this warming-up power of togetherness, the child learns not only to listen, but to obey and to respect people who are old. S/he also learns to actively participate in all activities of the community, i.e., to work for others. Above all, it is at this stage that the child is introduced to high-level knowledge related not only to our universe, but also to life, death, and the concept of *kala ye zima* (being/living and extinguishing/dying) as a natural dingo-dingo (process) of life and change.

Through Kindezi the child also learns that the world in which we live is not an individual proprietorship. It is for life and, therefore, should be shared by all. We as "individuals," who like to think of ourselves with a capital "I," all come into this world as weak beings. We grow stronger and then we must leave the world as weak beings, just as when we came.

C. THE SÂDULU

We already mentioned above that sâdulu is a babysitting site or spot. We prefer these terminologies to the Western "public day-nursing center" or "kindergarten." While the Western kindergarten prepares the child for Western formal education, the sâdulu prepares the child for the whole of life in the community.

17

The sâdulu, or babysitting site, is not necessarily a hut (building). It can be anything which accomodates exercising the art of kindezi: a roof of an unfinished hut, a cleared-out site under tree foliage, or just a spot on open ground or a veranda. Here children are brought to join their ndezi, old or young. Old ndezi prefer babysitting under a shelter to protect themselves from the sun or rain.

Children of two years or older are left in the sâdulu with their nkuta (food) in the hands of the ndezi. However, generally this food/nkuta is kept in the babysitter's house.

Babysitters of children under two years of age generally do not perform their babysitting duties at the sâdulu, but rather accompany the breast-feeding mother to her workplace so that the child continues, when necessary, to be fed with mother's milk. This particular ndezi must know how to keep the child comfortably "moored" on her/his back and how to help the baby sleep. S/he sings a lot while playing the nsakala, a sort of hand rattle, to lull the baby. S/he knows how to hold the baby and what to do when falling while carrying her/his charge on a slippery place/road. S/he must act in such a manner that the baby does not bend backward (mînguka/yekuka). It is important to note that this ndezi or n'sânsi can only be verbally reproached, not slapped at all. For, say the Bakôngo, to slap the closest person to an infant is to beat the child itself. Even verbal reprimand of the n'sânsi or ndezi in front of a child may cause the child to become ill.

Children in the sâdulu spend their days running, discussing, playing ngânga (healer/doctor), chief, and imitating other community professions. They stay away from their parents as long as they are happy with their ndezi and peers, and have enough food and fun. They play and make their toys with materials found on the spot. They learn how to weave, crack palmnuts, cook, make pots, and play market. They learn a lot about signals, symbols, and body language. A straight look (kintungununu/kiswèswe), for example, tells the child to stop whatever s/he is doing. The child knows the meaning of each unusual movement of her/his parent's/ndezi's eyes, fingers, and face—and even a simple expectoration can say a lot. At this given signal, the child must act as quickly as possibly to conform her/himself accordingly.

Sâdulu, the babysitting site, is a moving school where community children not only meet their ndezi but where they also learn while doing. It is during this stage that the child acquires the most exciting experience of life, that of togetherness as a shared spiritual thing for the betterment of community survival.

NOTES

1. Mbôngi, which literally means "public council house," is the seat of the traditional Bântu, the most powerful communal political institution.
2. For more details about Mbôngi, read Fu-Kiau's *The Mbôngi*.

IV. KINDEZI AND THE SOCIETY/COMMUNITY

The Kindezi can only be perceived and understood through the social context of the community it serves as an art and a big social responsibility. It is through the role that Kindezi plays in the community that one can appreciate its importance in the dingo-dingo (process) of shaping African social patterns. The quality and personality of the ndezi/babysitter, make by influence the quality and personality of the child in the sâdulu and the community as well. Since it is the ndezi with whom the child stays all day long, the future of the child will greatly reflect the image of its ndezi, the main shaper of its personality. This is the impact of Kindezi, the art of babysitting, not only upon the child but upon the society itself.

The contribution of Kindezi in Bântu societies in general, and the Kôngo in particular, cannot be underestimated or denied. The role it plays in all aspects of community life is so great that it merits erection of a monument.

Without Kindezi, the African woman would never experience the great amount of freedom she enjoys. Nor would she occupy the position she occupies in matters of land control and economic productivity.[1] Contrary to the Western woman, an African woman is more farmer than her fellow man. The African woman, in this perspective, is much more self-entrepreneurial than is her colleague in the West. Here in the West, the woman is basically an employee to man's work. The African woman stays on her farm from morning to the fall of night.

Hers is a land work done without any male participation, thanks to the art of Kindezi. A mother with a ndezi (babysitter) is a winged bird; she can go wherever she is able to. This kind of freedom enjoyed by African women, to manage their own affairs was not discovered by Western women until recently with the women's liberation movement, which was, incidentally born as a result of the anthropological discovery of the Third World. In the West, the land is the domain of men only. In Africa, it is principally the domain of women, thanks to the role played by the Kindezi in liberating women from the house. And this is a new phonomenon in the West.

For centuries, African women were "kings,"[2] generals, farmers, boatwomen, fisherwomen, doctors, traders, and miners (in pottery fields) thanks to the earlier discovery of the Kindezi that allowed them to be free human beings. They did not need a husband's assistance to cross a road, a river, or to secure their presence on the farm. To rely on the man's/husband's presence, say African women, is to give credence to the doctrine of female inferiority, the foundation of Western male chauvinism. This doctrine has been proven to atrophy the female's potential as a mother and/or in other professions within society.

It is well accepted today that women in Third World countries are the best economists or managers in the world:

> Anyone who has spent time in the villages can testify that the world's greatest economists are the illiterate women, for somehow they manage to keep their families fed on what seem like impossibly small budgets. The problem lies at precisely the opposite end of the social spectrum, with the well-educated, well-paid, and well-meaning functionaries who are meant to attend to world poverty and the desperate hunger it causes.[3]

Women in Africa today are still running after their ndezi in order to free themselves to be able to do whatever pleases them for the betterment of their families in a neocolonial Africa in which they now have no say.

In many parts of Africa, because men have to work in mines (*Azania*), road construction (as in Transkei) is fundamentally the task of women. Such an astonishing enterprise would be impossible if Transkei ndezi did not take the responsibility of caring for children while their mothers work in road construction projects.

In its practicality, the Kindezi can be seen as a veritable agency for community social services. It supports social and economic activities of the entire community as well as of each of its members. Mothers need ndezi to leave their children with when visiting family members in another community or sick people in the hospital; when going to the market to trade the produce of their farms or to buy what their domestic needs require; when going to farm, to fish, to pick up mushrooms, to funerals, or to any other social event to avoid any cumbersomeness. The Kôngo culture prefers, for example, that a lady going to a wedding ceremony goes free without a child; otherwise, she will not enjoy the ceremonial dance because of the presence of the child. On the other hand, it requires that all mothers must somehow be provided with an ndezi so that, in times of land cultivation, no one could pretend to be unable to work because of the lack of a babysitter. Today, the whole African continent is starving because, among other reasons, most of the ndezi have gone to school[4] and there is no substituting service for the traditional Kindezi. The lack of ndezi in the community due to the change of the system of education has reduced the capacity of production of foodstuffs among farmers (women). Mothers, like fathers, have chosen to cross their legs, to breast-feed their disquieted babies, and listen to peanut politics. Consequently, the whole continent is "eating" politics and dying a strange death.

To sum up, one can say that Kindezi has, at once, a social, economic, and political role to play in the community. Each of these roles has a unique objective: to serve the community and protect its youngest members.

A. SOCIAL ROLE

The art of Kindezi is an agent of social, cultural, and educational formation. It is the Kindezi that provides the most basic elements of cultural concepts to the child. At the sâdulu (the babysitting spot/site of care) the child learns its social relationships with others. S/he learns how to address adults in a respectful manner. The ndezi tells stories and the children, in circle, listen, clap, repeat, join the teller in chorus, laugh, and cheer. Much more, the ndezi has also to organize the children for games, dances, or dramatics. Here, clearly, the Kindezi takes a leading position in the oral system of education among the Bântu. The ndezi teaches the children how to make toys with *makaka* (a sort of grass), *bipôpo* (mud-dynamites, mud-balls), and many other things.

This Kindezi teaching takes a more animated form by the introduction of songs in the process and many *kûmu*, "motto words." This process is one of the most common in the teaching of Kindezi. Singing as a babysitter is an open and very challenging process. The ndezi must know what s/he sings for the child. The song must be explained in case its form is archaic and unintelligible for the child and other ndezi. The ndezi teaches simple songs that captivate the curiosity and the attention of the child. Through songs the ndezi teaches them the concept of sharing and its value for the community as expressed by the following song:

Wadia, wadi'e
Tala nkubu nâku
Nkubu nâku e
Lumbu kabaka
Ngângu e
Ngângu ziviôkele

While eating
(Better) look at your peer
Your peer
The day s/he might own
How smart (may s/he appear)
Very smart

23

By the same process the ndezi leads her/his children to the river for a bath. A very simple and enjoyable song is struck up. The ndezi sings the words and the children respond in chorus by singing *yô*, an esoteric way of saying *înga*, meaning "yes." They continue to sing as long as they are on their way to the river as expressed by the following song:

> *Mwèndo yôl'e*
> *Yô*
> *Mwèndo yôl'e*
> *Yô*
> *Na bingulu-ngulu*
> *Yô*
> *Na bintaba-ntaba*
> *Yô . . .*

> Going bathe
> Yea
> Going bathe
> Yea
> With little pigs[6]
> Yea
> With little goats[7]
> Yea . . .

Singing in the art of babysitting does not stop with this type of song. An ndezi can sing a lullaby (cradle song) that transfers, basically, a political system. We find this form in the following cradle song very popular among those Angolese people who were fleeing the Lustanian colonial system in Angola to embrace the paternalistic colonial system of the Belgian kingdom in the Belgian colonial empire of the Congo:[8]

> *E mu Leyo (tukwènda)*
> *E yâya mu Leyo*
> *E mu Leyo*
> *E yâya mu Leyo*

(Kadi) E Salazale
Wakitudi yo kwândi (nsi)
Se nsânsi ya gôndila[9] an'èto
E mu Leyo (tukwènda)
E yâya mu Leyo
E mu Leyo (tuwîla)
Yâya mu Leyo
E mu Leyo . . .

Hey! to Leyo[10] (we shall go)
Now then! Mother to Leyo
Hey! to Leyo
Hey! Mother to Leyo
(Because) Well Salazale[11]
Has transformed it (the country)
To a lullaby instrument
Now then! to Leyo (shall go)
Hey mother, to Leyo
To Leyo (shall go)
Mother to Leyo
Now then! to Leyo (shall go) . . .

The above Zômbo's cradle song is a typical political song used to transfer a political message in the art of babysitting: Angolan people had to leave their country, and sang the song to prepare themselves for an anticolonial war, because their rich country, Angola, had been transformed to a simple toy to please overindulged children, the colonialists. The war had to be prepared from a neighboring country (the Belgian Congo) to fight against the fascist Salazar of Portugal.

Cradle songs are also used to remind the ndezi of her/his duties when the child cries or weeps. "Never forget," conveys the message, "the way in which the art of Kindezi is practiced in Kôngo culture." That is, in other words, that the ndezi should take the child to her/his mother (at her workplace) if at all possible; thus advises the following songs:

25

Mâma wankâmba
Tâta wankâmba
Mwâna kadila
Nda[12] *lândis'e*
Mu nzil'a Kôngo
E-e kayânga[13]
E-e kayânga
Nayendi kaka
Muna nzil'a Kôngo

Mother told me
Father told me
If the child weeps
Bring it (to the workplace)
According to the Kôngo way
    Taking care, dear
    Taking care, dear
Always do
In the Kôngo way.

Another group of Kindezi cradle songs are the one which are basically used as lullabies (*N'kûng'anwukudila*). These lullabies serve, not only to lull (*wukula*), but to praise or support mothers in general and especially mothers of twins, *ngudi-a-nsîmba*. The following two songs will illustrate:

a) A pure lullaby:

Wa, wa, wa
Mwâna wanlôngo e
Sangamani e[14]
Buta katominanga
Kala na ndezi âku e
Sangamani e
Wa, wa, wa
Mwâna wanlôngo e
Sangamani e . . .

26

Quiet, quiet, quiet
Oh! sacred child
Look at her/him
To be a happy mother
Should not one have a babysitter?
Look at her/him
Quiet, quiet, quiet
Oh! sacred child
Look at her/him

b) A cradle song of twins:

Bâna bèto bôle
Kayang'e
Ma ngudi e
Kayang'e
Bôle bayiza
Bâna
Bôle
Bôle
Kayang'e
Ma ngudi e
Bâna bèto bôle
Bôle
Bôle
Nsîmba na Nzuzi e
Bôle

They are two, our childaren
Taking care
Twins' mother
Taking care
They came two
(Our) children
Twins
Twins
Take care
Mother of twins

They are two, our children
Twins
Twins
Nsîmba and Nzuzi
Twins

There are also other Kindezi songs which are strictly health related. For instance, many of these health-related songs teach that it is dangerous for a child to weep excessively. Weeping, says the song below, increases the body's "heat" (temperature) and can cause *yuku-yuku* (fever). For this reason and others, the ndezi is instructed to keep children as happy as possible instead of saddening them or letting them weep all day long. Here is a typical health song:

Wa, wa
E mwâna bidilu èyi
Yambula bidilu biâku
Mwânu-wu
Ni bio bitwâla' tiy'èyi

Quiet, quiet[15]
What a weeping child
Stop your weeping
Baby
It will bring you fever[16]

The last type of songs that we would like to mention here are the songs related to social conflicts and/or deviations. These songs prepare the child for the fact that her/his social, cultural and/or political environment is not totally sane and free of tensions. As such, the child learns, from an early age, that living is a dingo-dingo (process) in which one must continually struggle for change, growth, and development, even though this change may not always be positive. It is the responsibility of the ndezi to introduce such a notion to the child so that s/he will accept the environment as it is—as an interacting (conflicting) one.

The song-legend below, based on the life of a social deviator, paints the picture of this type of song. This song-legend speaks about a lady who leaves her first husband. When back in her original community, she finds herself rejected by and living in isolation from her people because they have misunderstood what happened to her in her community by alliance. Her community wants her to be a lady of good stature. However, for some reason, her community refuses to give her the benefit of bringing this critical situation before the community Mbôngi.

One day, the "rain/flood" (a metaphor for a stranger who is passing by and sees her in her state of rejection) comes and hooks her (takes her away). She agrees to leave her community to accompany the strange man. With this stranger she begins a new family and gets rid of all the previous problems connected with her first marriage and her community.

Along the way to her new community, the lady finds two bells. One of these bells has no handle and represents her former "broken" life, that life she left behind. The other bell, which has a handle, represents her new "hopeful" life. Once she arrives in her new community by new alliance, the rejected lady goes to see a specialist-of-charm named Mwânda in order to have her *mâmbu* (problems) tied up in a "fetish," *Mpûngu*, so that they will finally be put to rest. Mwânda takes the bell without the handle from the lady and gives her in return a beautiful spotted cloth/wrap that will act as a wall between her past and present lives.

Mono ubabela
Batûngila nzo
Va ntèndo bènga
Niâmba bu kayôka
Kayôla bisa
Kayôla mîku
Ngièle kwâmi bând'e
Ntôtele ngûnga zâmi zôle
Ngûnga zâmi zôle
Mosi yatabuka dikôngi
Yatabuka dikôngi

29

Mpèni kwa Mpûngu a Tâta Mwânda
Mpûngu Tâta Mwând'e
Umpèni n'lele wa maleso
N'lele wa maleso
Ni wo nikinina' ku lôngo
Yakina-kina fiôti
Nto-nto-nto zawîla lôngo
Kiwo-wo-wo!
Ya Masâmba
Kiwo-wo-wo!

Rejected
One built me a house
Near the abyss
The flood came
Took pots
Took ladles
I then went lower lands
Picked up two bells
Of my two bells
One had no handle
The one without handle
I gave to the fetish Mpûngu of father Mwânda
The Mpûngu of father Mwânda
Gave me a dazzling spotted wrap
With the dazzling spotted wrap
I dance[17] in my marriage
A little dance
All "problems" of my previous marriage
Are soothed
With ya Masâmba[18]
They are all soothed.

The social dynamics of Kindezi as they are understood among the Bântu people are not only limited to the teaching of games, plays, and songs. Kindezi is a process that shapes the entire life of the child and, therefore, the entire life of the community. Through the dynamics of Kindezi, the child learns

30

that s/he is not an element outside the social body of her/his society. The ndezi, parents, and child are all parts of a great ensemble, the social ensemble (Fig. 4).

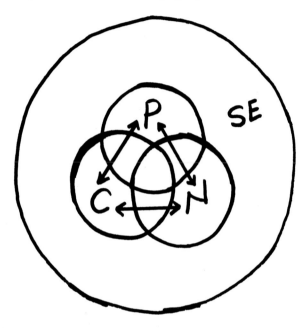

Fig. 4:   The child is not an element outside the social body of her/his
community:
C—child
N—ndezi/babysitter
P—parents
SE—social ensemble/community

All social relationships that work to tie all these societal elements together (parents, ndezi, and children) are in the interest of personal growth and community betterment. The more these social relationships are strengthened, the more the community is united and the more this community will excel in most of its activities. Thus, rearing a child becomes the responsibility of everyone in the community. "The child in the womb is one

31

individual's burden, but once out (born), it is everyone's child."
Thus, the survival of a child is the burden of everybody in the
community (Fig. 5).

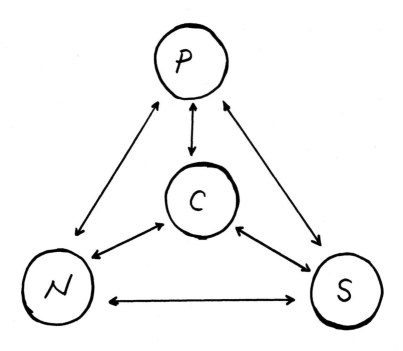

Fig. 5: The survival of a child is the "burden" of everyone in the
community.

Because of the lack of written documents for didactic purposes, the song occupies the position of choice in the traditional
Kôngo art of babysitting. Almost everything is taught through
songs because they are constantly repeated. It is through songs
and *Kûmu* (philosophical-didactical mottoes) that the Kon-

golese child learns the artistic beauty of her/his mother tongue. It is through songs and sayings that children learn that their community, with all its tensions and interactions, is a beautiful place to grow up and to be in. In the community, the child learns that creating a family is the sacred and wonderful responsibility of all. As such, all the children must remain in their community and grow up in the hands of its members. They will never be given away by the community, no matter what—either for money nor for parental incapacity. Children in the Kôngo society are not "things" to get rid of or "goods" to be traded. For the better as well as for the worse, the extended family must "starve" to save each community child. "I love to have children," a Mûntu will say, "because my community not only wants them but loves them"; i.e., all community members commonly feel responsible for children,[19] as the tale below suggests. The heroine, a young lady, prepares an audience with her family. She wants both blessings and permission to create a family of her own so that she can bear children and provide new members ("hens" and "roosters")—girls and boys for the community's needs (social, political, and military):

> *Ya Masâmb'e*
> *Ya Masâmb'e*
> *Mpèti mbèl'âmi*
> *Mbèl'âmi*
> *Yabudila mpâtu zâmi*
> *Mpâtu zâmi*
> *Yayaba ĝôngo diâmi*
> *Gôngo diâmi*
> *Yabaka nsûmba tânu*
> *Nsûmba tânu*
> *Yayenda kwè' batâta*
> *Ba' batâta*
> *Bampâna n'lele a nkelele*
> *N'lel'a nkelele*
> *Yayabikila mabène*
> *Bène diâmi*

33

Diatîta bu dilèmbo
Wuhu!
E nsusu ankènto
E nsusu ambakala
Wuhu!

Lord Masâmba[20]
Lord Masâmba
Give me my knife[21]
(With) my knife
I will carve my scoops
(With) my scoops
I will empty a pond
From this emptied pond
I will catch five nsûmba[22]
With these five nsûmba
I will go to my "fathers"
My fathers
Will give me a dazzling wrap
With the dazzling wrap
I will cover my breasts
(Then) my breasts
Will become erected and enlarged
Hurrah!
Then will come "hens"[23]
And "roosters"[24]
Hurrah!

B. ECONOMIC ROLE

Kindezi, the Kôngo art of babysitting, does not only deal with socially related responsibilities. In fact, the philosophical foundations of Kindezi stem directly from the social, political, cultural, linguistic, and economic aspects of Kôngo life. Babysitting for the community's youngest members is thus considered as one of the most popular and most acceptable activities used

34

in the Kôngo society to keep the physically disabled members active and productive for the economical betterment of the community as a whole.

To the Bakôngo, each community member is valued as a force of production. No matter what may be the physical state of an individual, the community must take responsibility for that individual's economic needs. For this reason, young and old alike are, through the art of babysitting, incorporated into the community process of production. They babysit for the community's youngest ones and, by doing so, not only free a group of the community's encumbered productive forces (young mothers), but also oblige the entire community to come to their economic support. By this process no one in the Kôngo culture is said to be a parasite of the community and its wealth. Everyone, by his/her means and ability, pays for his/her own survival.

A Mukôngo woman is generally an excellent farmer, thanks to Kindezi. Very often a women leaves her village early in the morning, coming back only after nightfall. She stays on her farm tilling the land, hoeing, sowing her field, cleaning, or harvesting. During all this time in the field she does not worry about her children because the babysitter takes care of them. Because of the support of the Kindezi system, the agriculture production of a Mukôngo woman has always been higher than that of the man.

In the past, this was especially true when fields and farming lands were safe for women to stay in and work for the whole day. With African neocolonialism things have changed. Now, women in the fields are experiencing some of the violence and abuse that women in the West have been experiencing in their city streets for centuries. And, because African men do not appreciate the working of the land themselves, the whole continent is experiencing a shortage of food. Women, the great "feeders" of the continent, are subjected to the same trauma as their colleagues on city streets in the West; they no longer feel secure in their fields because of irresponsible African revolutions.

As mentioned earlier in the introduction, the economic contribution of Kindezi is undeniable in African regions where agriculture is the key to local economic development. This Kôngo proverb is not a joke: *Mbôngila mwâna-wu yakângila babakala kilauki* (Hold this child for me so that I can help the men who are unable to arrest the madman). Thus, a woman freed of her baby/child is able to do everything. She has the capability of being a political and military force in her society in conjunction with her role as mother and economic contributor to the community. Freed of their children by the support of Kindezi, many women in the powerful kingdoms of the Kôngo became army officers and generals.

To rethink and to restore the Kindezi system in all its aspects is to restore not only the productive force of woman but also her political and military power as well.

C. POLITICAL ROLE

Kindezi plays an important role in community politics. This role can extend from a local to a national level.

Whenever conflicts and tensions exist within the community, the ndezi who is a member of the community, but neutral and free to contact any family where there is a child, can therefore be used by one side or another as an impartial observer and mediator. Acting in that manner, the ndezi becomes a means of reducing tensions within the community and between its members.

The ndezi, in her/his role as a teacher, is the first individual to raise the political consciousness of the child. This is accomplished primarily through make-believe, i.e., plays, games, songs, tales, and stories. It is through the ndezi that the child learns who is who in the community and who should be called what. S/he also learns certain basic elements of the social structure of the community, such as the kinship relationships and their heirarchy.

The political role of the ndezi is not limited to inside the community. It goes beyond the community frontiers. During the colonial era, the ndezi was used as a means of political resistance against forces of occupation.

One of the authors' fathers explained how Kindezi was used as a means of resistance against colonial forces in these words:

> Once territorial gendarms were sent in this region to contain the rising political forces of ngunzism.[25] Young ndezi who were not forbidden to play around the Belgian colonial military vehicles were drafted by Kongolese underground resisting forces to carry flasks filled with a very well-known, ancient, herbal formula used for warfare in order to secretly spray the vehicles with this powerful, penetrating substance. While the soldiers relaxed, the resisting forces, through the ndezi, did their handiwork. When soldiers came back to their machines and tried to drive, it was a disaster! The soldiers threw themselves on the ground, tearing their clothes in order to disentangle themselves from the mysterious piercing agent. Quickly, a medical team was rushed in to investigate the 'virus.' The team itself was hit with the mysterious attacking agent. The agent remained unidentified by the oppressive agents and local people laughed. It was finally decided by colonial authorities that the forces of occupation should be withdrawn from the area. In this way, Kindezi was successful in providing the community with an important political and military victory.

NOTES

1. In many parts of the African continent, the land is literally the domain of women.
2. We prefer this term to "queen" because queen does not necessarily mean political figure (chief, leader, ruler) of a country. Most queens (as labels or figureheads) are just like the rest of the women, while a king is always a political figure, a "ruler." Besides, in the Kôngo culture (base of the study) the term *n'tinu* translated for "king" is for both male and female "rulers."
3. Nick Eberstadt, "Hunger and Ideology," *Commentary*, 1981.
4. In Africa, the colonial philosophy of education requires that all schools of autochthonous origin be built away from communities (villages) to ensure not only the detribalization (brain-washing), but to facilitate the Westernization of the continent.
5. From Fu-Kiau, *N'Kôngo ye Nza yakun'zungidilia*, (Kinshasa: ONRD, 1969), p. 28.

6. Heavy (fat) kids/children.

7. Turbulent, restless, or unruly kids/children.

8. Today's Zaire.

9. Common variant *bôndila*, "to lull, coax."

10. Deformation of Léo (Léopoldville); today's Kinshasa.

11. Deformation of Salazar, the Portuguese dictator who was also the colonial ruler of Angola.

12. Slang; a shortened version of *wènda*, "go."

13. The infinitive is *kaya*, "to sit up, look after, watch over"; "to share."

14. This phrase is sung while raising the child up above one's head. In other parts of the country, this line is substituted by *vwema Mbadio* (Be quiet, "unnamed one").

15. This can also be substituted with "listen."

16. Literally, it says, "It increases the body heat."

17. I make a spell/charm.

18. The name of the new husband.

19. Unfortunately, with the invasion of capitalism and its concepts in our lands, this sacred social responsibility of the past is being thrown out in order to weaken the African social system.

20. Of *sâmba*, "the one who clears way," "the decision-maker," or "the social green-light switcher."

21. The word refers to the Kôngo sword, *Mbèle a lulèndo*, the insignia of the throne. It represents power, right, authority.

22. A sort of silurus, sheat-fish.

23. A metaphor: meaning "girls."

24. A metaphor: meaning "boys."

25. Political-religious movements (prophetism).

V. CONCLUSION

Kindezi, the art of babysitting, although one of the least-known fields in the acadmic world, has greatly contributed to the way our world is run. Without it, agriculture would have been unknown in many parts of the African continent prior to the colonial era. In fact, the colonial economy itself would have been impossible to realize if there had been no Kindezi. It was Kindezi that freed the hands of African mothers for use as *kiniemo* (free labor) and subsistence farming to support family budgets, which were impoverished by the extremely exploitive pay scales of colonial systems.

To rethink and restore the art of Kindezi would be to liberate a great productive force in society and to recognize women as equal to men. This process would also serve to unveil the woman's structure as an economic, political, and military power. Thus, to reinvent Kindezi would mean rearranging also the entire social substructure of the community. When we speak of Kindezi, we speak of an institution that affects community life as a whole. The philosophy that is at the root of the art of Kindezi argues that in order for human beings to understand the child, the adult, the community, and the totality of human life, it is necessary that we enter the world of the child, because human beings who are adults are merely the grown images of what they were as children. Dewey, Montessori, Piaget, and many others became famous philosophers and educators not by examining grown-ups, but by attempting to know the child in its world. What the childhood of a generation is will be what that generation becomes in its adulthood. A ruined childhood is a ruined society.

Nations, politically speaking, are children too, and leaders are their babysitters. When the babysitters become unaware of their social, cultural, and political responsibility, the life of the child in their hands can be endangered. What is true for the life of a child is also true for the life of a nation. When leaders of nations are politically illiterate and irresponsible, nations are ruined and destroyed morally, culturally, socially, and economically; worse, their inhabitants are transformed into birds without wings. We are thoroughly convinced that politicians should not take lightly their responsibility regarding child development, for to do so is to jeopardize their nation's future.

The art of Kindezi, *briefly described here, offers the reader an understanding of the art of babysitting as it was when it flourished among the Bântu people, especially in the Kôngo.*

We now know that most social and psychological problems[1] that afflict the community (violence, rape, robbery, drugs, murder—especially in industrialized societies) are, in many cases, problems related to the social and/or parental carelessness vis-à-vis the childhood of its youngest members. If the earlier childhood experience proves devastating to the later experience of adulthood, it is, then, very important that world communities pay great attention to Kindezi, the art that shapes the child's experience in its earliest stages. The community must know the state of mind of its ndezi (babysitters), especially when they are old and have a static or fixed experience to transfer. This fixed experience may sometimes be a negative one and can have a negative impact on the psychological state of the child and its subsequent adulthood.

A mentally sick ndezi cannot be an effective "artist" (babysitter) to those who are the hope of the world community of tomorrow. A babysitter should even be mentally healthier than the child's parent(s) for her/his role is more than a job with a certain pay (as in the case of the West) or a responsibility with a certain kibwanga,[2] "reward/recompense" (as in the case of the Bântu/ Kôngo). The responsibility requirement to the ndezi is to be a pattern (role model) of future patterns. Likewise, politicians and other leading figures of nations (who are "babysitters" to their systems) must mentally be in good health because a mentally insane lawyer, for example, cannot be a good defendant or judge, nor can mentally sick psychiatrist be a good therapist. Both can affect the sanity of an entire society. Insanity among the world's many decision-makers is a very dangerous thing. It can lead to any kind of disaster.

It is our hope that this study of Kindezi, the art of babysitting, will serve as a positive role-model for enlightened babysitters throughout the world and stimulate the world of business to rethink the conditions of the work environment to include Kindezi as an integral part of its functioning.

NOTES

1. Many of these problems are under way at the moment we are writing this study. Now Western technology is in the process of what we can basically call here "the children made alienated and insane at their conception" by fathers and mothers whose existence is only known by a few, through files, in laboratories and sperm banks. These children could be the most unfortunate, psychologically unstable, and dangerous in tomorrow's society.

2. In the case of ndezi, this reward is generally *bundezi*, the ndezi's reward, which may be a gift from the parents to the ndezi.

280121-100-17-60W